Moving to Excellence

(A Pathway to Transformation after Grief)

Robin Chodak

Creator of the TET Approach

ISBN-13: 978-0-9987088-1-2

Library of Congress Control Number: 2017917412

Editors: Gina Donaldson, Rennie Selis

Printed in the United States

Website:www.robinchodak.com

Table Of Contents

Acknowledgements

My heart is filled with gratitude for the inspirations that I have received on my journey. It may have been a book, a stranger, a friend, a song, a movie, or a hidden message from spirit. The positive messages that inspired me came from many sources.

I give enormous thanks to my spiritual family. Some of you have prayed for me over the years and some just recently. You all know who you are! Your prayers are powerful and they have aided in the manifestation and success of this book. Thank you from the bottom of my heart. My prayer is that you will be filled with even more excellence in your life.

I thank my husband Gerry for always showing his love and support to me. We have travelled this wonderful journey together uniting our souls in harmony and experience the beautiful life we have been given. Yes, I believe you can have more than one soulmate!

Lastly and most importantly, I am grateful to God for putting the desire in my heart to create this work. I am humbled to be a vessel to inspire others. The divine spirit within me has guided my path to transformation and provided everything I need to bring this message to you!

Introduction

Writers who write books understand the importance of a title. Sometimes it comes first and then the book evolves and other times the book is written then the title emerges. Let me tell you how this book title came to me. The words appeared to me before I even knew I was going to write this book. They appeared on a white stone. I don't mean that I was walking down the road and tripped over a stone with words written on it. Although that would be absolutely amazing too! It would also be believable because my life is filled with mystical experiences.

I was the one to write the words with my own hand on the stone, but my logical mind was not in use. It happened at a gathering called a "white stone ceremony." This is a spiritual ceremony where the participants do a meditation and then ask God or their higher power to give them a word or words for the upcoming year. You are instructed not to make them up or force them into your mind; instead you are to let God's spirit or your higher power speak to you. Every year has been a different experience for me. Once an entire phrase came to me but most times only one word. This particular year two words entered my subconscious mind. First, it was the word "excellence" and I wrote it on the stone. I thought I was done, but then the word "moving" came to me and I wrote it on the other side without questioning. They seemed strange as they always do initially but then the true meaning always gets revealed during the year.

I knew the words would lead to something amazing because the ceremony was held on 1/11 and the number 1 has been a very powerful guiding source in my life. If you study numerology you know that "1" is a power number. Any dates or times with 1 or 11 have been significant to me and always turned into great things. It was tragedy that awakened me to those numbers and it was tragedy that brought about my transformation. I knew the meaning of those words would be a big deal for me. Especially since 2017 adds up to 1 (2+0+1+7=10=1) and I had already claimed that 2017 would be a year of excellence for me. I had no idea what those words meant and jokingly said to my husband when I arrived home, "We may be moving." I knew not to be too hasty or literal, therefore I didn't start packing! Although I certainly didn't know that I would be writing this book since I was in the process of writing another one. A week later Patrick Dahdal the founder of Transformation TV contacted me. The laws of attraction were at work because I didn't seek Patrick out, instead he found me through LinkedIn. Before meeting him I had already set my intentions on reaching a million people with my message of hope and transformation. I had been thinking about it over the last year. I didn't know who Patrick was but felt that I should talk with him. An interview was scheduled and the following week I joined his team. The interaction came about because we have like-minded intentions about transformation and that is the reason I am writing this book. Plus, appearing on transformation TV would make reaching a million people even more likely!

You are reading this book now because of the laws of attraction. For those of you who haven't heard of this law, it means like attracts like. In other words, your thoughts will attract others with similar thoughts. At this time there is something in your realm that desires to hear and put into place the ideas that I write. They may be new ones for you, but you are ready! I am glad you are here with me because this is where transformation occurs. You will change the collective consciousness one thought at a time to create transformation in yourself and in the world.

Three weeks after my meeting with Patrick I noticed the white stone that sat on my bathroom counter since 1/11. When I looked at the words I knew they were meant for the title of this book. For weeks the words on the stone floated around in my head like a canoe on a semi-calm ocean. My logical brain didn't think that readers could imagine excellence with loss, suicide, tragedy or grief in their lives. Every day I metaphorically jumped into my canoe as the waves brushed up against it to listen for the words to become my title. Then one day the ocean was completely calm and the words just flowed into my mind. It was the same way I heard the words for my stone, they whispered in my subconscious thoughts, "Moving to Excellence, (A Pathway to Transformation after Grief)."

In all honesty I was intimidated initially by those words for my title because excellence and grief didn't seem to go together. I know that if you are in the throws of grief then excellence is the last thing on your mind. You probably don't ever think it's possible. In fact, the title may have evoked some negative feelings in you yet you were drawn to this book. That is a good sign. Some people will have passed it by because their consciousness was not ready for it. But you have not and there is a reason for it.

The title made sense to me because I understood it. Why? Because those words are my personal experience that I can share with you. I can't write about what I don't know but I can write on what I do know. I can write about grief because I was introduced to it early in life and the worst of it was thrust upon me when my husband died by suicide in 2005. Yet I know now how to live an excellent life because I have been transformed!

In my teachings you will hear how a white stone ceremony can begin the process that leads to your excellence. I want you to get ready for it now by searching for a white stone or one on which you can write. It doesn't need to be the exact color white, for example it can be a light colored stone that you find on the beach. Once you find it put it in a safe place and available to use in one of my video sessions.

I have learned not to ignore messages from spirit and it led me to create the Think Excellent Thoughts **(TET)** approach that I will teach you. It's the steps I have used over the years to get to the place of living a life of excellence.

Chapter 1: Who Should Read this Book?

Before we begin I want to warn you that this book may not be for you at this time in your life. In fact if you have recently lost someone you loved to suicide or from a tragedy or you are in shock then put this book down now. It is not meant for you yet. But it will be later! Do not continue to read it because your emotions are dripping with shock and confusion like a soaked beach towel hanging over a railing. Your mind will not absorb the content. I know this to be true because I was in that exact state of no absorbance when my husband died by suicide. In fact, I was in shock and didn't think my life was worth living. If this is you at this time then I recommend you read the book I published about grief entitled, "Be Gentle with Me, I'm Grieving." It is available on Amazon in Kindle format and in paperback. I suggest you read that book and then come back to this one. Also, the good news is that you picked this one up and there is a reason for it. But put it down now and come back to it a few weeks later after reading my other book.

Because I do understand grief so well and I am concerned for your well being I want you to answer this question before you continue; *did you seek help after your loss?*

If you answered yes, then go ahead and continue reading. But if any time you find yourself not ready to understand this content, then put it down and come back later. There will be a time that you will desire to continue this book and your conscious mind will be ready to absorb it. It will be the time that you desire to move toward excellence and then you will begin to transform your life. I am glad you are taking this journey with me. My thoughts and prayers are with you.

Also, I want to mention this book is not just intended for those who have suffered grief. It is for anyone who is ready for transformation. But I talk about grief because it was the pathway that created mine. You may have been on another path of some kind that has caused you to want transformation. It may have been an addiction, a divorce, a financial setback, a health issue or anything that has left you empty and devoid of your true self.

My goal in creating this book and my teaching segments is for you to realize that you **CAN** move to Excellence after a grief experience or at anytime. You may not believe it at this moment but just stay with me and continue reading. You will hear things presented in ways you may never have heard before.

I am going to tell you about myself but not just yet, because first I want to talk about grief. Stay tuned and you will hear my story, which will inspire you to achieve excellence in your life.

You were drawn to this book for one of the following reasons. Either you had a grief experience, or you want to know more about excellence. Or you are just a curious person and curious about my message. Curiosity is a good quality because it leads to awareness and awareness leads to self-discovery and self-discovery can lead to excellence.

If you picked this book up because of grief it is likely that you feel no one understands you and you want to be understood. Or you feel stuck and want to get "unstuck." Either way, you have come to the right place because now you have a chance to understand grief better. Be grateful you found this and that you are on your way to create excellence in your life.

If you want to feel validated in your grief this is where you will do it. Or maybe you have experienced some excellence in your life already but would like more. Perhaps you have never entertained the idea of excellence at all. Maybe you think it's far fetched for you. Yet part of you knows it's possible and therefore the reason you are reading this book. I believe books have energy wrapped inside each page and they come to each one of us at the exact time they are needed. It has happened to me throughout my life and always brought to fruition that which I was seeking. Words jump off the paper and become infused with energy and power to transform. This book has come to you to help you begin to make a change. It is because you are ready to move to better things in your life, yes even excellence! One of my favorite quotes is by the 13th-century poet, Rumi, "What you are seeking is seeking you."

So Why is this Important for you Now?

One reason is that grief may have already done some serious damage to you and affected your health in adverse ways. Maybe you gained some weight or swung to the other side of the pendulum and became anorexic. Perhaps you live an isolated life, or you turned into a curmudgeon. You don't need to inflict any more damage on yourself, and the truth is you are not getting any younger. Every day passes by very quickly and if you're not moving forward, you are likely in a stuck state or moving backwards. Time waits for no one. Now is the day for you to make a shift. It's time to find your excellence.

A MYTH I want to dispel is that most people don't ever expect someone who has suffered extreme tragedy and especially suicide loss to excel. In fact, grief wants you to believe that to be the truth. It wants you to accept that you should be happy that you can make it one day at a time. Yes, it's important to do so but there is so much more. Grief tells you to be satisfied that you got yourself out of bed and put not just one but both socks on your feet. Don't get me wrong; this is a big deal when you are in the throws of grief and in shock. Yes, it is progress, but the bus doesn't stop there! It wants you to get on it and ride to grander places in your life.

How do I know these things? I know them because I experienced them. Many days it took an exorbitant amount of energy for me to get myself out of bed. But I have survived and moved beyond that place into excellence and so can you. That's the reason I am here and the reason you have found this book. And believe me, there is a reason!

There is something inside of you that has sparked a desire for greater things in your life, for something excellent. At this moment you probably don't realize that there is excellence in you and that it wants to thrive! Trust me; it's there!

Grief wants you to believe many false things about yourself. It's like a large magnifying glass making every little fault of yours bigger and bigger. How could it ever let you believe that you could move toward something good or be something bigger than your existing pain? The only picture you see of yourself is one that is inflicted with pain and immobilized on a large screen. It's actually a still frame. It has stopped you in that one moment of your life when tragedy happened. You believe that is the way you should remain. That is the **myth** that must be shattered. Some of you who have suffered great tragedy believe that you should not have excellence in your life. This idea is wrong and meant to be rejected. Take that idea and throw it out the window and let it vanish into thin air.

Don't think grief is holding you back from excellence. It's not. There is something else that is. I shattered the **myth** and so can you. I learned how to do it and I can help you uncover for yourself what is keeping you from your excellence.

I talk specifically about suicide because I have had first hand experience with it from my husband's death and hear stories from my clients. All of us are embodied with unique emotions that bind us such as anger, shame, or depression, etc. Guilt was the one that continuously threw darts at me. In fact, it was relentless, and it actually found its way into my shoulder blades to cause excruciating pain. I visited the chiropractor week after week to have electric impulses charge through my back to get some relief. You must realize that negative emotions are filled with negative energy, and they search for a place to reside. The energy of guilt needed a home, and it found it in my body. Guilt made me believe I had done everything wrong in my relationship with my husband. A voice chanted in my head, *if you loved him enough, he wouldn't have killed himself.* Have you heard similar voices? You are not alone. The good news is those voices can be changed.

I know that if you are a parent reading this you may have an overwhelming sense of guilt when your child died. You believe you should have protected and sheltered him or her from any pain. Guilt makes you believe you must live with that emotion for the rest of your life. It wants you to think you failed as a parent and that's the reason your child died. Again, this is an all-consuming lie. You could not shelter your child from everything in his or her life. This would not allow them to grow and expand and become the person whom you loved and raised. His or her choices were made, and you couldn't have changed them. The only person you can truly shelter is yourself and your emotions. Do you think your child would be angry if you excelled and lived your best life? I believe they would want it for you just as you wanted it for them. Your ability to excel in life doesn't diminish the love you will always have for your child. Don't let grief lie to you any longer!

Guilt is the most destructive emotion that latches on to you. It is filled with low energetic vibrations and venom that keep you in a stuck state. None of us are responsible for the choices anyone else makes. Guilt will constantly throw into your face everything you ever did wrong in your relationship with the deceased. It will drag out the movies, books and photo albums from your past and make them today's news. But stop and think. How then do you justify the situations with great parents, great spouses, great relationships, and great lives and the person still ended his or her life? I have just created an argument against your way of thinking. You must understand that it was your loved one's pain and their choice, not yours.

Suicide and unexpected sudden deaths such as murders and accidents are much more complicated than normal death. We accept normal death because it is a natural part of the circle of life that can't be disrupted, redefined, or changed. But when it comes to suicide and tragedy our brains have a hard time accepting death. It's because we want to make sense of something that is senseless in our minds, therefore we take on an emotion to make us suffer.

You still may be asking why should I listen to Robin? Ask yourself if the previous methods you've tried helped move you to excellence. If not, then it's important to keep reading. Don't be fooled by those who say that you must attend a certain university to achieve excellence or be a member of a specific organization or pass a particular exam. This is all false thinking. Those are not the things that will bring excellence into your life.

Maybe you haven't experienced grief in your life yet and that is awesome! Or maybe you have, and you have already processed it. Perhaps you are already moving toward excellence. That is awesome too! Regardless, this is for you now!

Chapter 2: What is Grief?

Here I am once again seeking you out. I will latch onto you and suck the blood right out of your veins. I will bring you to near death. I know that is what you want sometimes, but this would be far too easy for you. This is my job because you don't understand me. I will do this over and over again until something changes. ~ I am Grief

I know that sounds very harsh to many of you, but If you have experienced grief like I have then you know it's the truth. I know many of you reading this have lost a loved one to suicide and I want to say to you that I am very sorry for your loss. Suicide is unlike any other form of death and adds many more complications to the grieving process.

I am here to share some SECRETS with you in this book.

SECRET #1: Grief is not what you think it is.

Most people think grief is the worst emotion they will ever experience. They consider it horrible. I am here to shatter that **myth**. When you have lost a loved one to suicide you probably agree and can say it was the most horrific experience in your life. Yes, absolutely, the loss you experienced was horrific, this is true, but grief is not.

16

I want you to begin to think about grief differently. In fact grief is the mechanism that can change your life. It's transformative and will move you in directions you never thought possible. Some roads may be good and some bad. But if you learn what I did about grief, you will experience roads that lead to excellence.

The very reason we encounter experiences is to learn from them and then to share them with others. I am honored to share mine with you and my hope is that you will not stay stuck in your grief but will become transformed in positive ways.

While I suffered through grief, I did a lot of things wrong. And when you let grief take control it will do nasty things to you. I know because it did it to me. But then I put a stop to it and made a 180-degree shift. And that is when the magic began.

Grief will impose many ideas, emotions and behaviors upon you. It will take up residence in your body. It will make you melt away to nothingness while it creates its own frozen statue of the person that was once you.

You will no longer recognize yourself as you gaze at your reflection in the mirror. You will look deep into your dark sullen eyes for some semblance of yourself, but it has vanished. You begin to hear voices in your head. They are sounds and words you despise. Your muscles become tired, and you can't sleep. Your body no longer belongs to you, so you don't care what happens to it. So, then **what do you do?** You want some relief and will try just about anything. You indulge yourself with food. You drink too much alcohol. You take prescription drugs. You take illegal drugs. You search for love anywhere you can find it. You wake up next to someone and wonder how you ended up in his or her bed. Does any of that sound like things you have done? You are not alone because most everyone does them to get some relief. Unfortunately, none of those will help your grief for very long.

Why don't those methods work?

Because they are just Band-Aids and the repercussions can be tiredness, weight gain or loss, liver problems, drug addiction, sexually transmitted diseases and the worst is more heartbreak. When you started down the path of using those remedies you probably never imagined the debilitating results.

Many believe that those are solutions for their pain. I am sure you agree that those are the wrong methods to deal with grief. But you do them anyway, often with regret. Don't be so hard on yourself because you are not alone!

Some of you have tried other methods, which are conventional and widely accepted such as psychotherapy and psychiatry. I am not claiming that those are wrong or bad and I advocate seeking help. But it is not the end-all answer. It is a start, and there is so much more needed. I realized I couldn't live my life chained to my therapist's chair. If you are not careful you can feel tied to the chair and glued to the past or in a daze from anti-depression medication. It is easy to feel trapped and believe there is no way out of your pain.

After doing most of those things myself to get relief, I learned that they were NOT the answer. I had to learn the lesson the HARD way. But the good news for you is that you don't need to nor should you! Read on and I will tell you what I have discovered.

Discoveries:

1) Don't be deceived; grief is a best-selling author on tragedy. It makes you pick up its book over and over again to re-read your story. It wants its words to stay in your waking consciousness all the time. The sole purpose of it is to keep you stuck in a time warp as your past is relived over and over. It wants to inflict every cell of your body with pain and sorrow.

2) Grief enters your house in the middle of the night like a thief and steals all that belongs to you, mainly your inner peace, your soul, your sanity and your hope. Grief hates when you reach out to others for help because it is jealous. It wants all of you all of the time.

3) Grief knows more about you than you do. It knows your long-forgotten secrets and the things you tried to bury. It is the hidden part of you that lays dormant. That is until the day arrives to shatter all your insides to shards of glass. It's the day you suffer extreme loss.

4) Grief wants you to believe that your life will never be good again, that it's over and that you will never find someone to love or be loved by another. It wants to make you feel like you are damaged goods, and no one will ever want you in their life.

5) Grief wants to make your loss be your identity. It wants to steal your true identity from you, and it wants you to believe that loss is your life story. It wants you to believe that the tragedy that has happened to you is all that now exists. That is another lie. Yes, it is true your identity has changed in some way, but your tragedy is not YOU. For me, when Steve died, I no longer played the role as a politician's wife or a married woman. Your roles have also changed. But it doesn't need to be a bad thing. In fact, you can create a new and better identity for yourself.

6) Grief's biggest and most insidious lie is to make you believe that not living in overwhelming emotional pain everyday is enough for you. It lures you into the belief that if you have been able to function in your life after loss that it means you have excelled. Either you have gone back to work or gone back to some old familiar routines, however, you barely exist. Grief makes you think that this is progress. But really you are only a mere shadow of who you are meant to be. Beware; it doesn't ever want you to believe there is so much more, that is, unless you learn how to tame it.

Can you relate to what I have just described? Has grief entered into your life? If you are reading this it probably has in one form or another. If you haven't experienced it yet, shout hallelujah from the mountaintop and be grateful that you have stumbled across this book. It can be your lifeline for when it does intrude upon you because no one escapes it. If you live long enough you will experience it. I can help you get the knowledge you need and not be tricked by it.

Many people who offer help will accept your getting any level of relief from your grief. Do you want to accept it? Is that really enough? I am here to shatter this myth. Mediocrity is not the answer. Excellence is!

You have just learned some secrets about grief, and **do you know what?** You can use them to your advantage.

Chapter 3: How Do I Know about Grief?

You may wonder how I know so much about grief? Let me tell you my story. It started when I was young and I wrote about it in, "Be Gentle with Me, I'm Grieving." I will begin in the month of September 2005. My day started out like every other workday. The coffee pot brewed its dark roast bean for my morning java to give me a jolt. I needed it to get my day started at 6:00 a.m. I jumped right into multitasking as I sipped my coffee, rode the stationary bike and read something inspirational for 45 minutes. Then I showered, dressed, and put on my makeup. This was my daily routine for 10 years while I was married to Steve. Incidentally he was my soulmate. We met at the right time in our lives after failed marriages, fell deeply in love and married eight months later. I know it sounds crazy to marry so soon after meeting, but we had a magical encounter and there was something greater than ourselves at work. It was the mystical magic of the universe! We knew our meeting was divinely planned to awaken us to experience a spiritual oneness and the miracle of love.

On this September day I went to work as usual. But it didn't end in a usual way. In fact, eight hours later, everything for me changed in that one moment when time ceased to exist.

My life seemed to shift to someone else's story. It couldn't possibly be mine since I had no chapters written for this type of tragedy. Mine already had grief and suffering, but this "book" was filled with pages of horror and shock without any remedy chapters.

September 14, 2005, I came home from work to find Steve dead. He had shot himself in the head, not once, but twice. I was the one to find my beloved's lifeless body lying on our basement floor from his brutal act and I immediately fell into a state of shock. I thought I would never recover from that devastating moment when my world turned upside down and all hopes and dreams vanished. But thankfully I did and that is the reason I am now writing this book. That life-changing moment began to transform me, and I believe you too have the same capacity for transformation.

When I think of the grief experience, I think of oysters. I know that it is a strange analogy but there is a reason. Incidentally, I love to eat oysters, but I didn't discover them until six years ago. They are actually a metaphor for surviving and transformation. Maybe that is why I love to eat them so much! They are a reminder of my journey. Interestingly, not all oysters get afflicted with a painful grain of sand or other irritant. Yet, the ones that do begin to create something beautiful despite their pain. The sand that gets stuck between the oyster's shell and mantle is very painful. The oyster protects itself from it by creating layers of nacre. The nacre substance usually creates the shell, but because of the unexpected sand the oyster's job is to create layers of nacre as a protection. Over the years the nacre builds up and within three to seven years a beautiful pearl is created. The grain of sand that once caused pain was turned into a beautiful pearl. That is transformation and excellence! Despite all the pain I suffered from Steve's death I have turned my life into something beautiful, just like the oyster. The same can happen to you.

The message I have is that you can become a beautiful pearl and be proud of your story. You don't have to stay stuck in your grief. You can move much, much further beyond it toward excellence. Your life changing moment can transform you in ways you never dreamed possible.

Does any of this make sense to you or do you feel that grief has dug its claws far too deeply into you and won't let go?

Answer the following seven questions to determine if you are stuck because of your grief experience.

1) Do you have more problems sleeping at night?

2) Do you find that you now blame yourself for things you have done, and others have done?

3) Do you find yourself overeating, drinking or self-medicating with drugs or alcohol more often?

4) Did you stop your exercise program?

5) Do you feel your emotions are more frequently out of control at times?

6) Do you more often isolate yourself from others?

7) Do you find yourself constantly thinking about your deceased loved one and become sad and depressed or feel other negative emotions?

If you have answered, "yes" to more than three of these questions then you are likely in a stuck state. But remember, you don't have to stay in it. Be grateful you found this book. Keep reading because it will be the catalyst to move you from grief to excellence.

Chapter 4: Three Steps to Process Grief

This chapter is for you if you haven't processed your grief. I give it as a gift to my clients and Facebook followers and now it's here for you. If you have already processed your grief, you can skip this chapter. But you can't move forward toward excellence until you do. There are three things you must do to begin the journey. Maybe you have done some and maybe not. But it's important to check in and determine where you are on your journey.

1. Seek Help.

2. Receive Love.

3. Trust yourself.

1) Seek Help

Don't make the mistake of thinking that you can handle your grief alone especially if it is related to suicide. You most definitely need help if you are in a state of shock and are suffering from post-traumatic stress disorder or are just plain stuck.

Many times, you are stubborn or you let your ego get in the way to make you think only the weak seek help. Actually it is quite the opposite. It takes courage to do so. Yet, many of you don't get it and it stems from a variety of reasons. Fear of facing your reality is one of the biggest. It was for me. Fear will hold you back from many things in life due to your false perceptions. I know that it is easy to want to deny the reality that your loved one is dead for as long as you can. Seeking help forces you to face the truth that he or she has died, and you are left without them.

I understand fear because it kept me hostage in my house. I didn't want to go out and be questioned by anyone about my husband's death. There is a stigma associated with suicide, and I felt as if everyone would judge me. I didn't want to be identified as *the wife whose husband died by suicide.* I feared people would think I was a bad wife, or we had a bad marriage. It was my own perceptions that caused this errant thinking. You may have felt the same way. At the time, my mind was in a state of confusion, and I couldn't think clearly.

My heart ached and I became depressed. I actually thought about ending my life so I could join my husband. Fortunately, there was someone who recognized that I needed help. I had to suffer prolonged emotional pain because I didn't get the help sooner. But I have learned from that, which is why I am here to help. You are here at the right time. Don't ever think it is too late to get help because it is always available.

I received psychotherapy, grief coaching and attended a suicide support group. I found that being in a room with others who shared the same type of loss as I did helped me to feel safe and not judged. They allowed me to express my feelings of anger, guilt, sadness, etc. In the absence of those environments, I felt isolated because no one could understand what I was experiencing. The group helped me validate my feelings.

I know that it's not always possible for you to attend support groups or therapy and that is the reason I created my Facebook page (www.facebook.com/suiciderecovery) and became certified to coach others on their journey. Whether you coach with me or visit my Facebook page you will have a safe place to share your feelings.

Seeking help is the first step to begin your recovery. Don't come up with excuses such as you don't have time, your kids need it more than you do, or no one understands you, etc,. These again are all false perceptions that stem from fear. And what is fear? Fear is **F**alse **E**vidence **A**ppearing **R**eal. Are you going to let fear rule your life? Here is another way to think of fear. You can **F**ace **E**verything **A**nd **R**un or you can **F**ace **E**verything **A**nd **R**ise. I chose the latter and I hope that you will too! Excuses will keep you from starting your journey of recovery. Don't let them; instead RISE to your excellence. You are worth it.

For many of you it is scary to go down an unfamiliar path and easier to live in the pain. But this is not a long-term solution. If you continue to deny the truth and live in misery you will never recover or move toward excellence. The choice is really up to you.

2) Receive Love

The second step needed in your recovery is the ability to receive love. This may sound strange to you. It may be easy for you to give love, share love, or spread love, but you may have a hard time receiving love. Actually, that is exactly what you need most when you have just lost someone you deeply loved.

Do you feel your heart has been torn into a thousand pieces and that it will never be whole again? Do you feel numb and believe that love doesn't exist anymore for you? Are you filled with anger or guilt? Do you feel you hate yourself, God, and everyone else? I certainly did and those feelings are normal for someone who has suffered an unexpected loss, especially from suicide.

Hopefully, there will be others around you who want to show their unconditional love by caring for you in loving ways.

They don't have an agenda and don't expect anything in return. Their only concern is your wellbeing. They won't judge you about how you are handling your grief. Their desire is to be available to you when you need them. They want to help you in any way they can. It can be such things as bringing you a meal, taking you to the grocery store, doing household chores for you, taking you to the park or just coming to your house to sit with you. For some of you it is hard to accept those acts of kindness because you are the one who is always giving. In doing so you often neglect yourself. This is not the time to be self-sufficient. You need care now more than ever and this is the time to begin to learn how to accept it from others. Put to rest your old way of thinking and open your heart to receive love.

It is easy to want to push others away and stay in your grief. But this will not help you begin your journey to transformation. It only hinders you. Do not deny someone the gift they receive by giving love to you.

Until you can learn to receive love you will never be able to give love. It works like a ping-pong match. Once the ball (love) is sent to you, then you must send it back if you want to stay in the game. You must be willing to give out what you want to come into your life. This doesn't apply only to love. If you want a friend, then you must be a friend to someone else. If you want kindness, then you must give kindness. If you want understanding, then you must offer understanding to someone and so on. It is the universal law or theory behind "giving and receiving." If you give, then you shall receive. Another way to look at it is that if you don't receive you have just stopped the energy flow. **Do you really want to do that?** Keep it flowing by receiving and giving! As you do this you will bless others, and you will also be blessed.

This will start your journey to love yourself unconditionally. If you don't really love yourself, you can't genuinely love others. Your loss may have enhanced feelings of self-loathing that existed even before it occurred.

Tragedies have a way of bringing up many things from our past that we have hidden away for a long time. The time is **now** to open the closet and bring those secrets out from behind closed doors. This is the beginning of self-discovery.

3) Trust Yourself

The third step on your journey is to trust yourself. What I mean by that is to learn how to listen to your inner voice. This may not be something that you are accustomed to doing. You may not even know where to begin. As I said before recovery is a journey of transformation and self-discovery. You can become entirely transformed in positive ways you never imagined.

Many people don't know how to listen to the "still small" voice inside of them because of the noise that is always in their heads. We get distracted in many ways throughout the day and often we can't remain focused for very long.

After Steve died, I didn't think my brain worked the way it once did. My job as a systems analyst required intensive analytic thinking and focus. But my mind was in a state of flux and my thoughts ran wild like caged animals trying to escape. I couldn't do my job or hold my attention on anything. If I was going to keep my career and survive, I realized I needed to learn something new to calm it down.

That is when I began to do things differently. One thing I did was to start meditating. Don't get frightened by the word meditate. There are many people teaching various methods. For me, meditating is the ability to find a comfortable place to be silent and clear as many thoughts from my mind as possible. Any place that is peaceful to you will suffice. It may be a park, the beach, a forest, a room in your home, anywhere that is free of disturbing noise. I found a quiet beach to sit. My method was to stare at the water and listen only to the sound of the waves. My focus was to synchronize my breath with the crash of the waves on the shore. If a thought other than that came to my mind, I allowed it, but then let it go. I didn't get angry with myself when it drifted to other thoughts. As I continued with this practice the interfering discourse of my mind became less and less, and I felt calmed. It was then that I began to get in tune with the thoughts that bombarded me throughout the day. I became more capable of deciphering them and trusting the ones that were best for me.

My decision process became easier because I began to trust my inner self. If I needed an answer about something I would ask myself, *will my actions create good for me and for others or will they cause discomfort?* I learned how to listen to my inner voice. It didn't happen overnight; it came with spending time alone in silence. There are tools that assist in the process. Your progress is based on your desired outcome. I wanted peace in my life and spirit, and I set out to get them and therefore I did. You can too. Follow these three steps: 1. Seek help, 2. Receive love and 3. Trust yourself, to begin the process. No one can accomplish them for you. It must come from your own heart's desire. I assure you that if you do them with a willing and loving spirit you will get positive results. You will then be on your journey of transformation and self-discovery and ready for the next steps.

Chapter 5: Who's in Control?

The question you should ask yourself is, **who is in control?** Is it grief or is it you? Actually, it is both at different times. Grief is a very misunderstood emotion. Grief defined by freedictionary.com is: "Deep mental anguish, as that arising from bereavement, or an instance of this. A source or cause of deep mental anguish." When you are in this type of emotional state you shouldn't need to stuff down or deny your deep mental anguish. You feel intense pain from the severing of a relationship with whom you were deeply connected. You feel a part of you has been torn away and grief is a natural, normal way to feel. Don't let yourself or others believe that there is something wrong with you if you grieve. You must do it before you can move to excellence.

If you love deeply then you shall grieve deeply when your loved one is gone. Therefore, it's important to grieve and take the time that is needed. Don't be fooled by others who say, you will feel this way the rest of your life or your pain will always be a part of you. The question I want to ask you is, "Why would you want the pain to always be a part of you? Wouldn't you rather have your loved one's memory and positive energy always be with you?"

An important step for you is to begin to think of your loss differently. I want to challenge your thinking with this exercise. Step outside of yourself for a moment and see yourself as the one who died by suicide or died tragically. Now, look from where you are to those left behind. See your spouse, children, parents or friends. Would you want those you loved to feel responsible for your death? Do you want them to suffer for the rest of their lives? Would you want them to think their life is over or have them devalue the life they have been given? Of course not! If you love someone you ultimately want the best for him or her.

Now step into your loved one's shoes for a moment. I want you to think about them very carefully. Do you think your loved one wants you to have a good life? Or, do you believe that they want you to suffer? We often talk about how much we loved them and vice-versa but are we acting in the way that shows it? It doesn't matter if they are alive or deceased. If love is truly involved in a relationship, then the desire for others to suffer does not exist. Causing one to suffer is the opposite of love. There are many feelings, states and attitudes that describe love.

Let's re-examine the complex and abstract nature of love. Philosopher Gottfried Leibniz hit the nail on the head when he said, "love is to be delighted by the happiness of another." To me that is one of the best descriptions of unconditional love. Let us delight in others' happiness. In order to do so we must become non-judgmental and unselfish. So challenge yourself and ask how much love do you want to show your loved ones who are alive or deceased? Why should "delighting in others' happiness" ever stop? It shouldn't if you believe love is more than physical. I warned you that this book would cause you to think differently. I believe you are ready and that is why you are reading it. Continue to keep your mind open to new ideas. It will ultimately lead you to possibilities that bring transformation.

Let's break this concept into smaller chunks. Do you believe in love? If you answered, *yes* then continue. Do you believe that love never dies? If *yes*, then continue. Did you and your loved one have a loving relationship? Do you see what the result of this is? If you answered *yes* to all those questions, then there can't be a long experience of pain in your life. Yes, you will have a grief experience, but you should not have a stuck state. If you continue to live in pain, you have created a "disconnect" from the love you shared with the person who has died.

Love is the highest vibration that exists. Jesus taught us to love one another. Rumi said, "Goodbyes are only for those who love with their eyes. Because for those who love with heart and soul there is no such thing as separation."

Buddha said, "True love is born from understanding." I believe Steve wanted me to understand love at the highest level and to know that our union always exists, but not in the physical realm that we once knew.

Because love exists, your loved one would want you to experience happiness in all aspects of your life, even though they have chosen a different path. They don't want you to experience the emotional angst that they felt. After all, that is the reason they ended their life. They were in unbearable pain and their minds could not think logically. But you can and you do! It is your choice to honor them in love by living an excellent life instead of living in pain. In fact living in pain is a violation of who you were designed to be.

Does that make you think differently? I hope so. I hope that it opens your mind to a new way of thinking about your life as you live it and about the love you will always share with your deceased.

You still may be thinking that I don't understand your pain. Well, don't think I do not. Of course I do! I lived with grief and I read posts everyday on my Facebook support page of those who have lost loved ones to suicide and I also coach clients. I hear many stories of pain. What I do is to help you understand that your emotions are normal. But they should not be the identifier of your life or control you. If you want to honor your loved one you can do so by moving toward excellence. This does not in any way negate the love you have for him or her. In fact it enhances it.

Steve taught me many things while he was alive during the short 10-year period we had together. There were many mystical, magical moments in our relationship, and I am grateful for what I have learned from them. But it hasn't stopped; Steve continues to teach me in his death. He taught me about love and ironically one of the songs that he wrote and played before he died was called, "It's all about love." Maybe he knew he was going to depart this earth because he played it for me several weeks before his suicide. I believe he played it to teach me that love, in fact, never dies. Just as the strumming of a guitar creates sounds that fill our ears with delightful melodies, so does the love of those we've lost continue to surround us. Steve and I shared an unconditional love for each other, and he wanted me to carry on that love. I was meant to love and be loved, and I am living in love. I honor him by doing so. You are no different; you can do the same.

Grief has the capacity to build strength in you. But beware! You must not let it deceive you. When it grabs hold of you and thinks it has control that is when you must take over. You must thank it and say to it that it will always be your friend and be part of your life experience. But kindly inform it that you are now in charge because you are moving beyond it toward excellence. Grief understands this process when you are in control. It is then that you will move to create the best possible expression of yourself.

You may still ask; *can I really move to excellence after tragedy?* The answer is *yes* and there are things that you must do. Do not be deceived into thinking this will be easy. It's not. It takes work. Everything that creates positive results takes effort. So, if you don't believe you can do it, then put the book down now and stay where you are. But don't expect anything to be different in your life. You can stay stuck and be a victim or you can choose something different. You may not like the sound of that, but it's the truth. It's your choice and you have the power to shift your thinking. Grief does not have power over you! I believe in you, and you are here with me because you have the fortitude and desire to change. Doing so will mold you into a wonderful tower of triumph. You will be an example and a light to many.

Now for those of you haven't suffered grief, after reading this you are probably feeling very grateful, and you should! But the same question applies to you, "Who's in control?" Are you in control of your own life? You probably automatically say, "yes." But are you really? Do your emotions and negative thoughts control you? Is your life filled with drama? Are you unsatisfied with your relationships or with your job? If you answered **yes** to any of those then you aren't really in control. Your default mode network is! It's the part of your brain that is filled with all those beliefs that are putting you in unsatisfactory places. You create your reality with your words, thoughts and feelings. If you want excellence, it's time to use words that heal, bless and prosper you. It's time to take control and begin to **TET**(think excellent thoughts).

You must begin to give serious thought to what you want to experience in your life. There is no need to settle for less, instead, why not settle for more? Become definite about the good you want in your life. There is a saying I've read that says, "Shit Happens." I propose we change it to, "Excellence Happens!" Start to think of yourself as the writer of your story. This means you get to create the "book" exactly as you want it. Begin to imagine the scenes in your story. Make them excellent. If you have already experienced bad stories, why do you want to create more of them? I know some of you have gone to hell and back already. It's your time to write a new, excellent story. For those of you who haven't experienced grief, don't wait for it to be forced upon you. Create the character in your story the way you want now! It's your new identity. I did it because of my grief experiences, but I made sure that my story this time around would be good. I had enough bad already! You can do the same. You have the power and are in control of your life. You are given free choice everyday to think excellent thoughts and imagine your dreams coming true.

Chapter 6: What is the TET Approach?

I am sure you must be intrigued with the **TET** approach that I have referred to in this book. You can't move toward excellence unless you use this approach. It is the premise for it. It made sense that **TET** mystically came to me because that is exactly what I do all day long. In fact I used it before I knew it existed. I used it at various times as a child and it was what saved my life after Steve's suicide.

My transformation began on a beach in 2006 and that is the reason there is a picture of me on this book cover. Spirit directed me to choose that particular picture of myself the same way it directed me to choose the title for this book. The beach is where I put **TET** into action. You will hear about it in my training videos. You will find that all things begin to piece together like a puzzle when you **TET**(think excellent thoughts).

Have you ever worked on a puzzle when you were a child? If so, you probably started with an easy one or one that you could eventually complete. Didn't you find such pleasure as you stood back to view your completed masterpiece? Did it motivate you to work on a more difficult one? It did for me. The sense of accomplishment gave me incentive to begin a more challenging puzzle. Those 500-piece ones took time and effort, but it was worth it to see the finished product. Creating a life of excellence is like putting together a puzzle. Each piece is another step on your journey and the result is a completed beautiful work of art and a sense of accomplishment. It's a metaphor for life! Our accomplishments create the desire for more. Excellence does the same. When you have it in your life, you realize you can achieve it and then you want more of it! The universe is assisting you in the process by giving it to you.

For some of you, thinking excellent thoughts means having more money, and there is nothing wrong with that idea. Although, many have been taught that money is the "root of all evil." That teaching is explicitly wrong, and a myth meant to be broken. It was passed down from the bible, but the bible says in 1 Timothy 6:10, "The love of money is the root of all evil." Money in itself is not bad. It's only when you love it to the extent that it causes greed does it become a problem. Somehow the wrong translation spread, and people accepted it to be the truth.

Have you heard the parable where Jesus speaks about money? It is found in the New Testament of the bible in the book of Matthew, chapter 25 verses 14-30. It's about three servants given talents of valuable gold or silver disks. I will paraphrase it for you. A master went on a journey and entrusted his wealth to three servants. He gave five talents to one, two to the other, and one to the last. The man with five immediately put those to work and made five more. He doubled his holdings. The man who had two did the same. But the man with only one talent dug a hole and hid it in the ground. The master returned from his journey to settle his accounts with them. The one to whom he had given five said, "Master, you entrusted me with five talents, see, I have gained five more." The master replied, "Well done, good and faithful servant! You have been faithful with a few things; I will put you in charge of many things. Come and share your master's happiness!" The man with the two talents said, "Master, you entrusted me with two talents; see, I have gained two more." The master replied, "Well done, good and faithful servant! You have been faithful with a few things; I will put you in charge of many things. Come and share your master's happiness!" The man who had received one talent only had one to give back to his master. The master told him he was wicked and lazy, and he should have put it with bankers to earn interest. He took the talent from him and gave it to the one who had 10.

The story is told in the bible because our God, or Higher Power wants all of us to have abundance. For everyone who has he will be given more and it's our inheritance to have abundance or an excellent life!

In order to receive you must understand this concept. You do so by having the right kind of thoughts and they are thoughts of excellence. The man who was lazy and didn't know what to do with his talents received nothing. The other men knew what to do with them. They knew how to create excellence. They made right choices that produced good results. You now know what to do. Begin to **TET** (think excellent thoughts) about abundance and money and it will come to you in some way. It may be as simple as finding a $5 bill on the street!

In order to move to excellence, you must begin to Think Excellent Thoughts! It makes sense, right? It is what started me down the path of transformation and I have used it for over 10 years. It's not something that anybody taught me, it erupted from deep within my spirit during times of grief. It was necessary if I was going to move beyond it. You may not know where to begin, but I will teach you. It only takes one little thought of excellence to create another. Each thought escalates to another just as when you are riding an escalator. One moving step rolls into the next. The thoughts in your mind are the same. You must be aware of the negative ones. If not, you will become caught up in a vicious cycle of destructive behaviors. If this happens to you it's because you don't know how to change your thought patterns. Some of the most influential forward thinkers such as Gandhi, Mother Teresa, Thich Nhat Hanh, Norman Vincent Peal, and James Allen have known how to do this. They all have been examples to me and to many others.

I am using **TET** at this very moment as I imagine people walking around wearing t-shirts that say, "Do you **TET**? I do!" I also imagine people signing their text messages with **TET** instead of LOL. People want positive messages of hope in their lives, and many have been called to give them. I am a vessel to bring one to you. **Why?** Because I understand it, live it, feel it, breathe it and created the approach to share with you. I am passionate about living an excellent life. What are you impassioned about? It's time to begin to think about these things. I challenge you to do the following exercise.

Write down at least three things that will create excellence in your life. If you have more than 10 start another list. The reason to put them on paper is because studies have shown that people who write down their goals have a higher success rate of achieving them than those who don't. The act of writing will cause you to think deeply about what you want to accomplish. Don't say to yourself that you will do it later. That is procrastination. This is your time to do something for yourself. Give yourself the freedom to do it. Remember, if you don't write them down then the success rate is lowered.

1)

2)

3)

4)

5)

6)

7)

8)

9)

10)

If you were honest about what you wrote your list should include those things that you are passionate about doing and that is why I asked you to think about them. It's your passions in life that bring you joy.

If you are going to change your thinking you must learn how to do it. You must become like a child and learn the way they do. They learn by repetition. This means you must repeat what you have learned if you want it to stick. This takes practice just like everything else where success happens. Once this practice becomes a part of your life your mind will not hold space for negative thoughts for very long. If they do enter in, you will become aware of them quickly. I will give you an example of what happened to me recently when I had some negative thoughts. This is a reminder that I am not perfect nor is anyone. At one time I thought that everyone who created wonderful how-to methods for us were masters at them all the time. That is wrong thinking. They are human just as you and I are, and they too have faltered. It's those challenges that allowed them to learn, grow and create their methods or approaches. That is a freeing thought in itself.

One important thing I have learned is, *don't beat myself up* when I falter in my actions or thoughts. Like I said earlier, when successful people *mess up* they get back on the bus and ride. In this case, I will say bike since it's related to my story. Anyone who knows me can attest that in addition to being a passionate tango dancer, I am an avid cyclist. One of the reasons I chose to live in Florida for seven months is to ride my bike almost daily, usually between 20-40 miles. It's the gift I give to myself to connect with my higher power, nature, and my inner spirit. It is a sacred time for me, and I often receive messages from spirit.

If you know anything about Florida weather, you know it can rain on a dime and then suddenly stop. The winds can also become brutal. Those are the days I exercise indoors. Last month the winds were as high as 25 mph with even higher gusts and typically you don't see people on the beach or out for a walk. The winds had been howling aggressively for several days in a row and the gym in my building was out of commission. My husband was going a little stir crazy as I was and said that he wanted to take a ride despite the wind speed. Because I am a small person barely over 100 pounds, I opted not to join him and told him the winds would probably blow me over. The next day the gym was still out of service, and my husband planned to ride again. I told him *no* again. But as soon as the words rolled out of my mouth, I realized that I had just limited my thinking. I was not practicing **TET** (think excellent thoughts).

The first wrong thing I did was to *make an assumption*. I assumed the wind would knock me off my bike. And the second wrong thing I did was to *obey the default network* in my brain that said you don't want to work that hard in the wind. But then **TET** kicked into my mind, and I said to my husband, "Wait, I'm going with you." You probably can guess the outcome, right? I didn't get blown off my bike and it was a great ride. Why? It was better than I imagined for a couple of reasons. Number 1, there were fewer people outside because of the weather, which made it easier to maneuver through the town and number 2, on the ride home with the wind at my back I rode faster than ever. I think I broke my record. Take notice of what happened. My limiting thoughts tried to stop me. But once I no longer let them the results were better than I could have ever imagined, even beyond my wildest dreams.

Due to that lesson, I will never let the winds stop me again, unless there is a hurricane! We must always maintain a level of safety for others and ourselves while we use **TET**.

I am grateful for small reminders such as that one. They keep me living my practice to **TET**. After all, I must be authentic and practice what I teach. The most important lesson is that it didn't take me long to become aware that I wasn't thinking excellent thoughts. Once you start the practice you too will discover when you are not using it. This is the reason your life becomes excellent because you live it with no limitations and beyond your wildest dreams.

I also want to remind you that the power of your thoughts is always at work and if you think negative ones, then the outcome from those will eventually come to fruition. I will give you another example with a bike story! Recently I was cruising down Ocean Blvd like I always do and literally out of nowhere a man crashed into me from behind. I was jolted to the pavement while his body catapulted over his handlebars onto the grass. I immediately jumped to my feet as if nothing happened and ran to check on him. He was moaning with pain, but coherent. I think he was shocked more than anything. After a few minutes he realized he was not badly injured and only had a few scrapes on his knees. I would not consider that a pleasant experience but I always choose to see the good in every situation. One was that many people stopped to ask if we needed any help or if they should call 911. It confirmed my belief that there is goodness in human nature always at work. The other was that there were no cars on the road when the accident happened. If so, they could have hit us and caused some serious damage and even death. The other plus was that we both wore helmets. In my opinion it's a death wish if you don't, therefore I always ride with one!

Please pay close attention to this next part. Neil, the man who crashed into me, told me he had biked for about 40 years and had many accidents, some of them off of mountains. He also said that shortly before our accident he had been thinking he hadn't had one in a couple of years. Those were his words, not mine. He also said he was lucky he wasn't riding his expensive Italian road bike. Instead, he had an old beat-up mountain bike. So, what do you think about that? No one in their right mind would want to create an accident for him or herself, not on a conscious level anyway. The accident wasn't consciously planned, but remember, thoughts are energetic vibrations and turn into form. And like I said, I was protected; nothing bad happened except for a bruise and a scratch. So, think about it and remember to pay attention to your thoughts. If you TET(think excellent thoughts) you will not be thinking about accidents. No one wants to create them, but they can occur when a person falls into a state of self-sabotage at the unconscious level. A point to emphasize is that it's also quite interesting that Neil chose not to ride his expensive bike on that particular day. This story was told for your awareness. Be careful what you think!

Think of examples in your own life. Do you constantly think badly of someone or negatively about certain situations in your life? Do you complain that things aren't working out for you? Well, guess what? This is a result of cause and effect. You can't expect good things to happen when your thoughts are negative. You must begin to change them. There is a universal law of cause and effect always at work, regardless if you believe it or not.

Have I convinced you to want to begin to **TET** (think excellent thoughts)? If you still need convincing, I will give you another motivating reason. People like to be around other people who **TET**. If you do so, then you spread positive energy that inspires others.

Recently, I heard my neighbor mention someone who always complained to him about the things wrong in the building. He said that he hated to be around this person and avoided him always. You see, my neighbor was already moving in the direction to **TET** and didn't want the negative energy around him. When people share their negative stories with me, I always tell them, *complaining should not be part of the story*. A light bulb usually goes on in their heads and they realize they must stop. Sadly, most people aren't aware they are doing it unless you point it out to them. If you begin to use **TET,** you will find that you are attracted to more positive people than negative. Don't be surprised if you lose some friends as you begin to transform. But I assure you that you will attract new ones.

There may be some of you who are thinking this sounds much too airy-fairy. It's easy to pass judgment on something you don't understand. I am not claiming that **TET** will prevent something happening in your life that will rock your boat. But I do claim that your perception of events will be different once you start this practice. I wake up every morning with a heart filled with gratitude for what I have created in my life, and I am happy to be one with God and one with the universe. This journey has led to my transformation. I didn't always think like this! You may also be led to a similar spiritual transformation if you so desire. One of my favorite scriptures is Romans 12:2, "Be ye transformed by the renewal of your mind." That is exactly what happened to me. The new thoughts that I put in my mind are what transformed me! The new thoughts were my **TET** thoughts.

My existence brings me joy; therefore, excellence is my state of mind, and it can be yours too! When challenges come you will have a different perspective. Again, I reiterate if a tragic event hits you out of the blue, your first thought will not be excellence, but your mind will be in a much better state to process your emotions. You will have a heightened awareness of everything happening around you.

When you first begin the process you consciously choose to think excellent thoughts, but after time passes you will do it subconsciously. Once you begin this journey the universe conspires to keep you moving in excellence!

Chapter 7: What is Excellence?

Excellence means greatness. It means being the best you can be at something. It's a sense of wellbeing. We all have excellence within us. You have it and so do I. Right now let's do an exercise. I want you to take a moment to think of a time when you did something really great in your life or something that made you feel very proud of yourself. It could have been a sports event, artistic event, something related to work or a personal relationship. Think of anything that made you feel good and you knew it was good. Stop now and think about it for a few minutes.

Didn't it cause a feeling somewhere in your body? You may have felt it in your gut or your chest, or maybe you had goose bumps on your arms, etc. Well, that was the excellence within you. You didn't need to dig too deep while reading this to remember it and perhaps you even felt it as you thought about it and let the memory absorb you. Why? The reason is that it's already within you. You had it then and you still have it now. But for some reason it has been pushed deep down inside of you. Grief and other unresolved issues can hide those feelings of excellence and make you believe they no longer exist. The good news is you can get them to emerge again.

The problem you have now is that you don't believe you have excellence and you probably were not taught to think you do. You were not taught to TET. Not many people told you to think excellent thoughts about yourself and others. Instead, most of us were told something bad or wrong about ourselves when we were children and we accepted it as the truth. If we learn something bad about another person we tend to focus on it instead of his or her excellence. The bad often overshadows the good. Sadly, this is not uncommon. Many of you spend all your time and energy focusing on everything that is wrong with you and the broken parts instead of the good working pieces of your life. If children were taught to think excellent thoughts about themselves at a young age I believe we would have a different world. It would be filled with more loving, compassionate, peaceful people. The good news is that it's not too late. You can start now!

You must remember when things are broken they can be fixed. Have you fixed random things in your house that fell apart or stopped working? I am sure you have and that is the reason super-glue and batteries were invented. Have you ever broken a bone in your body? Didn't the bone mend after specific care or surgery? Or have you had a knee or hip replaced? I have heard testimonials from people that say the new parts work better than originals. They claim they have a new lease on life and are living better than ever. They exercise more, move around more, become involved in new sports, and do things they never imagined before the injury or replacement. This is the same for you. You can experience more than you ever dreamed possible if you start this journey to excellence.

SECRET # 2) No thoughts are grandiose.

Are you diminishing your thoughts to small things instead of large? You must begin to think about what you really want in life even if it seems grandiose. There is nothing too big for the universe to handle. It's important that you begin to do so. I do. Nothing will turn into substance until you think it first. I think about this book as I am writing it now and imagine it as being a bestseller and reaching millions of people. I also think about you as you are reading it and I send out thoughts that you will be affected in positive ways and then I imagine that you recommend it to someone else. My thoughts keep the energy flowing. Does this sound grandiose to you? I hope not. Please stop now and join with others who are reading this and send out a positive thought about it. Let the thought be that this book will reach millions and change lives. You have just set the intention and the vibration has gone into the universe.

Let's watch together what happens in the future. I thank you in advance for contributing to the manifestation!

I want you to understand that the universe responds to our thoughts. It doesn't matter if they are yours or mine, or if they are negative or positive. There is always a response to a thought. You will begin to realize that there is another world that exists besides the physical. It is an invisible one or spiritual one that creates intangible things in your life such as love, wisdom, beauty, joy, peace, and health.

You must first have a thought before it can become a possibility or something real. Just as this book was initially a thought, now it is a reality. It has turned into substance. Your thoughts can do the same. How do you think others have succeeded? It started with their thoughts of success. This is what I want to convey to you. You must begin to think of your life as being excellent. Don't think about a past failure. It's done, it's over; you can't ever get it back. It's important to think about the here and now! It's time to **TET** (think excellent thoughts).

I like to equate the way the universe works to technology because that is a field I know. My degree was in computer science and I worked in that business for 20 years before I started this journey. I wrote hundreds of programs in many different computer languages. I started with the low-level language Assembler. But with the evolution of technology the languages changed to higher-level ones. It meant I needed to learn them if I planned to stay in my career. Our thoughts and brains are like computer languages, we must continue to think at higher levels. The universe is like a big computer taking in all types of data. It gives to you what you put into it the same way a computer reads the language of a program. If I wrote a bad program it would put out bad results or could cause the entire program to malfunction. As an analyst I needed to be sure that I wasn't writing any bad code. I certainly didn't want a malfunction in the company's financial systems. Nor do I want any malfunctions in my life, so I realize I must be clear about what thoughts I put into the universe! I do my part to keep the computer functioning by practicing **TET**.

It is important to understand the workings of your brain and know how to use it to your advantage. There is a default mechanism that works on autopilot when not engaged in cognitive tasks and often creates havoc, thus the reason for anxiety, worry and no inner-peace. But when you learn how to tame your brain then change begins.

Let me let you in on another secret.

SECRET # 3) There are only two things that you must have to move toward excellence.

Don't let others tell you that you must enroll in lengthy courses that cost thousands of dollars or travel to a distant land to achieve it. That's not necessary. The two things that I am telling you about are free. And the good news is that we all possess them. These are not only for the Oprah Winfreys or the Tony Robbins of the world. These two things were given to each and everyone of us the day we were born. In fact, we didn't need to do anything to get them. It didn't matter who our parents were or what their wealth was or their origin. You could have been born in a castle or a trailer; it doesn't matter because we all equally possess these two things.

I imagine your thoughts are racing like Mario Andretti's car competing in the Daytona 500. You will be surprised how simple the answer is....so I will let you in on this **SECRET**. The two things that you need to bring excellence into your life are **Mind** and **Spirit**. I know it sounds extremely simple. But most things emerge out of simplicity into something grand.

I have discovered ways to work with the mind and spirit that will lead you toward your excellence. That is the reason I love to coach and teach. Excellence is not limited to just a few, it is given to all. So why shouldn't you have it?

Do you understand that you are both human and divine? You have a divine spark within, and you are a grand cosmic being, so bring forth your true nature and let it work for you.

This is what **TET** will do for you. The reason is because the universe responds to your energy.

You will discover that as you begin to **TET** your life will change, and you will have so much more to offer to yourself and to others.

Chapter 8: Begin to Think Differently

I ask you to open your mind and begin to think differently about many things. Yes, this book is about moving to excellence but first we must talk about death. Why? Because for many of you reading this it was the death of someone you loved that caused your grief. It did for me too, thus the reason it created my transformation. Even if you haven't lost a loved one you may feel that your divorce, loss of a relationship or job felt like a death.

I tell you upfront now that if you don't process your grief or any blockages you can't move toward excellence. The universe can't bring good to you unless you release blockages. I will answer the question you are probably asking yourself. **Can I do it?** Of course you can. That is the reason you found this book. I did it and many others have too and so can you. But if you're not ready, then stop here! Read my grief book as I mentioned earlier and contact me if needed. I will continue to remind you because I want you to understand I do know the pain of loss and suffering. You must be ready to accept this challenge. Yours is to realize that your life is to be lived with excellence.

Understanding death will help you process your grief. You already have ideas about death that you have carried around with you your entire life. They have been molded into your psyche since childhood from family, teachers and religious leaders. *But what do you really think about it? Do you believe everything you have been taught? Are you afraid to challenge your thoughts?* It was necessary that I did because what I was taught didn't resonate with me after Steve died. I had to challenge my thinking and that is what led to my transformation.

After Steve died, I thought about death often, mainly *his* death. I couldn't grasp that he was once alive and suddenly gone forever as if he never existed. When my sister died, I didn't grapple with the idea as much because I assumed she was in heaven since she was a young person who became afflicted with cancer. She didn't live a long enough life to accumulate a lot of sins which some say will condemn you to hell. Therefore, heaven awaited her. But from some churches I attended I was told that those who took their own lives wouldn't make it to that place called heaven. Some believed Steve would burn in hell through all eternity. Haunting images of flames consuming his body and hearing his screams caused me to re-evaluate my thinking. I certainly couldn't hold that picture in my mind. He was one of the most kind, loving, giving men I had ever met. I had questioned what kind of God or creator would send him to a furnace room? I couldn't fathom that the man I loved would be tormented through all eternity; he already suffered enough pain in his physical realm. So, my quest for truth began and my ideas about God, life and death changed.

You may believe in heaven and hell or neither one. It doesn't really matter, but what does is that you come to terms with death. One thing we do know is that energy never dies, therefore our loved one does not cease to exist in some form. Only their physicality is gone, the part of them that we could touch, see, and smell, but their essence lives on. What do you believe about it? Do you believe that once a person dies that they are gone forever? It's important for you to think about these things and be open to new ideas.

I found myself consumed with anger about Steve's death. I wanted to blame someone, and God seemed the best source. I couldn't understand why he didn't stop the suicide. Steve was a man with faith; an active member of the church and he believed in God so I thought at the least God should have intervened. I also thought that God slapped me on the back once again. I had already been smacked enough times and thought I had done my penance for all my prior sins, but this made me think there was no more hope for me. Everything I thought I believed about God became overshadowed with confusion, so I decided to turn my back and walk away for a time. I left the church and had no contact with it for a few years. That happened to be the best thing to occur in my life because I cleared my mind of all the teachings I had absorbed. I discovered that my ideas about God that I had been taught were all wrong! And thankfully so! If you have felt the same, don't worry. It may be the best thing for you. God does not condemn nor judge. Instead, he is perfect being, perfect love, perfect source, and in everything and in everyone.

I write much about grief because, after all, that is the stimulus that led me to my transformation. It wasn't until I experienced the dark night of the soul that I had my spiritual enlightenment. I contemplated taking my own life to join Steve, but there was a divine source that said it wasn't the answer for me. In fact, an angel intervened on my behalf.

I believe we can experience our deceased loved ones in a new way. Have you had dreams about him or her? Did you ever see someone that looked like your loved one? Or have you met a stranger who reminded you of their character? Do you feel their energy near you at different times? These things have happened to me and some of you have had similar and more profound experiences. I call these gifts from the spirit world. I believe that our loved one's energy can only come to us when we exist in a realm of peace. They do not want to visit us if we are living in fear, pain, anxiety, anger, guilt or any other negative emotion. They already existed in the physical realm with those emotions so why would they want to enter near them again? It makes sense to me, and I have encountered Steve when I am at peace. I believe he is eternally using the **TET** approach.

Chapter 9: What's Next?

Now is the time to break the **myth** that you can't achieve excellence. You must believe that it is possible in your life. Let me give you some real life examples. Also, don't think that you are too poor and don't have the money to do it. Money is not what it takes. I will tell you what it takes. An example is the well-known U.S. actress, comedian, singer and writer named Carol Burnett. She had a long running TV show named, "The Carol Burnett Show." She wasn't born into fame. She was born in 1933 in San Antonio, Texas to alcoholic, impoverished parents. They divorced 5 to 6 years later. Carol and her grandmother moved to a poor town in Hollywood, California. They were on welfare and so poor that her grandmother often collected toilet paper from public restrooms because she didn't have the money to buy it.

Despite all Carol's setbacks she had a dream, and it was to go to college at UCLA (University of California, Los Angeles). It seemed a far-fetched reality at the time since there was no way she could afford it. But Carol kept believing and stating that she would somehow get there. She often imagined and role-played her future starting from the time when she was a little girl. Carol imagined herself going to UCLA, but she didn't know how it would happen. She held the thought and image in her mind. One day after graduating from Hollywood High School in 1951 she received an anonymous envelope in her mailbox for $50. Wow, amazingly, it was enough for her first year's tuition to UCLA. It was a miracle! Who sent it to her? There was no note, no explanation, just the money. She didn't know where it came from, but it didn't matter. This started her path to excellence, and she became a famous actress.

Carol Burnett is just one example of using the *power of thought* to move toward excellence. If she can do it, then why can't you? She didn't have wealthy parents nor come from a successful family. She didn't have special connections to open doors for her. She had the total opposite. Some would have deemed her a failure from the start. In short, she was an ordinary person just like you except she had visions of achieving excellence in her life. Don't make excuses that you have had more bad breaks than she. Her example of excelling can teach us many things.

You should not be asking; *will I ever move to excellence?* Instead, you should ask; *how can I do it?*

You may be saying, OK Robin, maybe you're right. I'm really not that poor, at least I can buy toilet paper, but nobody wants me even though I have talent. Well, here is a headline news flash; **you are wanted, and you have talent that**

someone needs. I will tell you another example of someone who achieved excellence. Do you know why this person achieved it? The reason is because he believed the newsflash. Actor Jim Carrey went from a dyslexic struggling young man to an amazing comedian and actor. He tells the story of how he would go to Mulholland Drive in California and sit in his car and look out over the city and proclaim, *everyone wants to work with me, I am a really good actor, I have all kinds of movie offers.* Guess what? He believed those things to be true. He didn't have them when he said them, but he believed he would get them. **When are you going to believe excellence is for you?**

One day Jim Carrey took it up a notch and wrote himself a check for 10 million dollars. He said it was for his acting services rendered. He folded it, put it in his pocket and five years later that money came to him by way of a film. No one thought the movie would ever make it big, but it did. It became the hit, "Dumb and Dumber." The rest of Jim's story is history. I am not claiming that you will receive 10 million dollars, but what I do claim is that it's not impossible if you begin your road to excellence. Who knows? 10 million may be in your future!

These things happened to a young kid who had challenges in his life so why can't they happen for you? I ask myself the same question. That is the reason I am writing this book. I am not a big celebrity yet but notice the operative word *yet*. I had a lot of negatives from the start in my life too, but I didn't let them stop me. Success can happen to me, and you should think the same about yourself.

You may be thinking Jim Carrey and Carol Burnett could achieve excellence because they didn't have suicide in their lives. This may be true, but that is not the reason. Excellence isn't reserved for those without suicide. In fact, some of my clients and many others have gone on to live excellent lives even after the suicide of a loved one or from other tragic losses, such as plane crashes and murders. Of course, they grieved but then they moved to a state of excellence.

Excellence doesn't always mean something grandiose or on center stage, although it certainly can. It's what you want to achieve. Another example is a woman named Gloria who was 11 when she lost her mom to suicide, which was over 50 years ago. At that time there were no Internet connections, iphones, social media tools, support groups or coaches to help her. In fact, the death of her mom was brushed under the rug, because "suicide" was not talked about during that time. The stigma was extreme. Gloria felt the sting and always lied when asked how her mom died even doing so on medical forms. It wasn't until she learned how to process her grief and move beyond it that she achieved excellence. Now she is married, has grandchildren and she became a successful playwrite. Many of her plays have been performed on stage. She has achieved the excellence she desired.

Another case is Dr. and Mrs. G.oodstein who lost their son in 1999. Their journey through grief led them to share their time and raise a large amount of money for AFSP (American Foundation for Suicide Prevention). They have created excellence not only for themselves but also for others with their generosity. They enjoy retirement living in Florida and have taken up new hobbies such as golf and art.

Everyone's degree of excellence is different. Don't think that once you feel you have excellence in your life that you have arrived, and you're done. We are never done! We keep *moving*, thus the reason for the word used in the title of this book. Once you start on the road to excellence it will continue to create more of it in your life. I already know that I have excellence because I feel it, see it, hear it, smell it, taste it and live it everyday. But that doesn't stop me. The road I am on is a never-ending path that keeps creating. You can be on that road too! Everything that you and I have become is the result of our thoughts and feelings. If you don't like what you have created so far, don't worry. You can begin creating excellence at any time. It starts with **TET**.

I ask myself, why shouldn't I get the chance to get my name and message heard like all the other big leaders in the world? I believe I should because I have a unique message. I don't hear many people shouting excellence from grief. I am presenting a new way to look at it. I believe it's a grand message and you are here with me because you have excellence in you. We can be pioneers at spreading it together. We can begin a movement of people who have achieved excellence because of it. We can become the leaders in this arena. This is not something fake or unattainable because this is about transformation. I have been transformed into excellence because of my grief experience and so can you. All of my heartaches, sorrows, pain and the horrific night when I found Steve dead led me down the path to my transformation

Chapter 10: What's holding you Back?

I want you to ask yourself the following question. Say it out loud so the universe hears it. Then answer it honestly.

What is holding me back from my excellence?

The truth is that the only thing holding you back is **you**! Once you begin to change your thoughts amazing things will begin to happen in your life.

You must realize now that your mind is going to rack up all kinds of ideas of how to hold you back. Some are fear of the unknown or low self-confidence, and they will shout loudly in your ears from a large megaphone. The more you hear those thoughts, the more they will continue unless you stop them. This is not your fault. It's what you are used to hearing. Don't blame yourself. This is and has been what's been put into your mind since you were a child.

The world would be a better place if we all began to think excellent thoughts. It opens the door for prosperity to come into everyone's life. Many things our society does inflict injustice onto others because it keeps people stuck in the way they think about themselves. Poverty is a perfect example. We classify people and name them into that group. They identify themselves as being poor and it makes it very difficult for them to move beyond this imposed identity. We don't empower them as a society to show their self-worth and all the goodness they offer. Instead, they believe that they need the government or others to take care of them. They are not taught to think excellence or prosperity, which is a state of mind and starts with one thought. What I have described all along is about positive thoughts and how they affect us, but the same holds true for the negative ones. Thus, this is the reason so many people live in a poverty state of consciousness. Nothing will change unless the thought does first. Only then can it turn into substance of something good. They may not get out of poverty overnight, but they can begin to move forward, and it starts with their thoughts.

Think of your mind as a garden. If you plant a seed for a tomato, you don't expect a cucumber to harvest nor will you get one. It's the same with your mind; what you put into it will grow and expand. Why would you think good will manifest if you plant negative thoughts?

I want to challenge your thinking again. You have a physical body, right? You are alive, right? Yes, you are. You are alive in your physical body, and you are 100% alive, right? Not just 50% alive. Science hasn't figured out a way to keep us half dead and half alive. So then, if you are 100% alive why shouldn't you live your life with 100% that is all yours and what you can achieve? Are you limiting yourself with your thoughts? I know it's hard to admit, but it's time to get into the mud and start building your new house. One brick equates to one positive thought. If you add one on top of the other you will soon have a new, beautiful structure!

As I mentioned earlier, many things hold us back and one of them is not doing the necessary work. If you work toward your goal, you will get results. First you must take some personal inventory to discover what is holding you back. If you have some negative emotions that you haven't resolved this could be the reason you are not living in excellence.

Take a look at the following short list and write next to the word the first thought about it that immediately comes to your mind. Don't sensor it.

ANGER_____

FEAR _____

JEALOUSY _____

DOUBT _____

GUILT _____

BITTERNESS _____

Now, look at what you wrote and think about the experience. I want you to notice any changes in your body.

Are you tightening up your muscles? Where do you feel sensations? Do you feel a jab in your stomach? Do you feel sharp pains? Has your breathing changed? The energy flow causes these physiological changes in your body and is a contracting energy. Negative energy contracts us and positive energy expands us. Think of a time when you felt joyful. Didn't you feel as if you could accomplish anything, and didn't you feel excellent? This is energetic expansion. It's as if you are larger than life. This is a feeling of excellence. Before you can begin to **TET** you must clear out unresolved emotions. It is up to you to determine if you are hanging on to any of them. I can't do this for you. Only you can. You must be honest with yourself and do the work. I have said all along that moving to excellence takes work!

Below are some questions to help get you started to uncover your negative emotions.

- Are you holding on to anger against someone?
- Do you have fears?
- Can you define your fears?
- Are some of your fears about success? We normally don't associate success with fear, but success brings about change and we often fear the unknown. You may worry that your life will change and you will leave others behind.

- Are you jealous of others for living excellent lives when you're not?
- Do you wish to be in someone else's shoes?
- Do you doubt that you can achieve greatness or doubt everything good in general?
- Does guilt still have itself wrapped tightly around your neck?
- Are you bitter against another person for something they did to you?

Those are just a few questions that you must answer honestly. Continue to ask them of yourself until you can answer them. Once you do so, then you can begin the process of releasing them. If you aren't able to release those negative emotions, you will not be able to move to excellence. That is the reason I said this takes work! You must deal with those emotions that you have bottled up in your life. Once you do and unscrew the cap the sweet smell of excellence will permeate the air for you to begin.

I want to close with one more story. It's about a man who was born in 1846 in Wales to impoverished parents. When he was three they immigrated to the United States and settled in New York in search of economic opportunity. Samuel had to work on the family farm at a very young age. At 14 he went to work in a sawmill, at 16 on a steamship. At 18, Samuel moved to Pennsylvania to work in the oil industry, which was booming at the time, but he was unsuccessful. He returned to New York to seek employment, and he saved his money for three years. He then returned to Pennsylvania where he invested his savings into oil. It was then that he began to create wealth for himself. At the age of 46 he established the Ohio Oil Company, which was later bought by the Standard Oil Company. Samuel M. Jones became a very wealthy man. How? He persevered and he had a certain way of thinking, which was an excellent way of thinking. In 1887 he became the mayor of Toledo, Ohio and was known for his declaration of the Golden Rule, "What I want for myself, I want for everybody." Wow, I greatly admire Samuel for his thinking. He did not have thoughts of greed. His were of prosperity and generosity.

I tell you that story because what I have discovered I want for you. I want you to create an excellent life for yourself just as I have. I am glad that you have found this book, and I hope you are filled with desire for excellence in your life. I believe you are, or you would have put this book down a long time ago. But you are here with me to the end because your mind and spirit want more. All you need to do is follow my **TET** approach. I developed it after learning and using it for over 10 years.

You have heard some important tidbits in this book to scratch the surface of my 10-step approach.

1) Commit
2) Remove Blockages
3) Process your Grief
4) Clean House
5) TET (think excellent thoughts)
6) Attitude of Gratitude
7) Do Acts of Kindness
8) Do Things you Love
9) Dream Big
10) Act

My teaching videos will walk you through each step and I will teach you step 5 that will enable you to begin to change your brain. You can purchase the videos on UDEMY by visiting www.Robinchodak.com.

If you are interested in one-on-one coaching to get you started on your journey to excellence visit http://robinchodak.com/coaching-sessions-robin-chodak/ to learn more.

Begin your journey today, you won't be sorry!

There is enough excellence in the universe for you!

Love and Light,

Robin Chodak

Certified Grief, Life, Spiritual Coach

Certified NLP Master Practitioner

Certified Reiki Practitioner

Certified Mindfulness Meditation Teacher